BLACK FLOWERS

POEMS

BLACK FLOWERS

DOUG RAMSPECK

LOUISIANA STATE UNIVERSITY PRESS ┃┃┃ BATON ROUGE

FOR BETH AND LEE

Published by Louisiana State University Press
Copyright © 2018 by Doug Ramspeck
All rights reserved
Manufactured in the United States of America
LSU Press Paperback Original
First printing

DESIGNER: *Mandy McDonald Scallan*
TYPEFACE: *Whitman*
PRINTER AND BINDER: *LSI*

Library of Congress Cataloging-in-Publication Data
 Names: Ramspeck, Doug, 1953– author.
 Title: Black flowers : poems / Doug Ramspeck.
 Description: Baton Rouge : Louisiana State University Press, [2018] |
  Includes bibliographical references.
Identifiers: LCCN 2017059283| ISBN 978-0-8071-6826-4 (pbk. : alk. paper) | ISBN
  978-0-8071-6827-1 (pdf) | ISBN 978-0-8071-6828-8 (epub)
Classification: LCC PS3618.A479 A6 2018 | DDC 811/.6—dc23
LC record available at https://lccn.loc.gov/2017059283

The paper in this book meets the guidelines for permanence and durability of the Committee on Production Guidelines for Book Longevity of the Council on Library Resources. ∞

CONTENTS

vii .... Acknowledgments

CONJURING

   3 .... Winter Fever
   5 .... Crow Hours
   7 .... Ancient Worlds
   8 .... Gravity
10 .... Diaspora
12 .... Notes on Beauty: *The Skull*
15 .... Ars Poetica with Heron and Dance
17 .... Fanfare
19 .... Feast and Famine
21 .... Skinny Dipping
22 .... Song of Praise

CLAIMING

27 .... Crow Art
29 .... How Humans Came to Love
30 .... Birthmark
32 .... Winter Schools
33 .... Dust Day

35 .... Divining Mud
36 .... The Body's Mud
37 .... Prayer for Stones
38 .... Bottomlands Departure
40 .... Dreaming of Golden Flowers
42 .... Feral Moon
43 .... Moon Letters

BURYING

47 .... Nomads
49 .... Unblessing
51 .... Wintering
53 .... Mother
54 .... Long Marriage
55 .... Nine Crows
56 .... Revival
57 .... Paper Skin
59 .... Touch
60 .... Black Flowers
61 .... Winter Snow
63 .... Mud Eulogies
64 .... Confession of Bats
66 .... Map of the World
68 .... Naming the Field

ACKNOWLEDGMENTS

Grateful acknowledgment is made to the editors of the following publications where poems in this collection originally appeared:

32 Poems: "How Humans Came to Love"; *Alaska Quarterly Review:* "The Body's Mud" and "Prayer for Stones"; *Barrow Street:* "Feral Moon"; *The Carolina Quarterly:* "Song of Praise"; *Ecotone:* "Dust Day"; *The Georgia Review:* "Ars Poetic with Heron and Dance"; *Kenyon Review Online:* "Nomads"; *Mid-American Review:* "Unblessing"; *The Missouri Review:* "Black Flowers," "Confession of Bats," and "Gravity"; *Natural Bridge:* "Divining Mud"; *New Madrid:* "Long Marriage"; *Nimrod International Journal:* "Crow Hours," "Moon Letters," "Nine Crows," and "Touch"; *North American Review:* "Naming the Field"; *Rattle:* "Diaspora"; *RHINO:* "Crow Art," "Revival," and "Winter Fever"; *Pleiades:* "Mother"; *Prairie Schooner:* "Dreaming of Golden Flowers"; *River Styx:* "Ancient Worlds" and "Wintering"; *South Carolina Review:* "Paper Skin"; *Southern Humanities Review:* "Skinny Dipping"; *The Southern Review:* "Bottomlands Departure," "Feast and Famine," "Notes on Beauty: The Skull," and "Winter Snow"; *Tampa Review:* "Winter Schools"; *Valparaiso Poetry Review:* "Birthmark," "Fanfare," "Map of the World," and "Mud Eulogies."

BLACK FLOWERS

CONJURING

WINTER FEVER

My father, in the hard gray
of winter, is kneeling again

and sliding the knife
from sternum to crotch,

blood welling like a dark liquid
oozing from a secret burrow,

intestines pouring onto grass.
Dead is dead, he always claimed,

adding that we might as well
toss him someday in a landfill

for all he cared, leave him
to feed the buzzards we saw

some days circling beneath
the stillness of low-slung clouds,

as though an end were little more
than a gathering in air, a few

serrated wings, a January wind slowing
then stopping in desiccated weeds.

The dead deer watches me
watching my father clean his knife

by wiping it against his jeans.
He told me once he planned

to die alone, to crawl into
the undergrowth beyond the barn

and listen to his breaths
grow more and more labored

then disappear, the way the body—
freed of the responsibilities

of common day—slowly devolves
into the perfection of pale bone.

Earlier I had watched him
carrying the deer on his shoulders,

four legs wrapped around his neck,
the way, when I was younger,

he would ferry me across
the living room then up the stairs.

CROW HOURS

Always we saw them in the trees by the river.
It was the summer the cutworms claimed

my mother's tomatoes, when a falling turkey oak
shattered our dining room window. The farmhouse

began crumbling around us: dirt caking windowsills,
bricks coming loose. And then the neighbor boy

drowned beneath the green bridge while collecting
crawdads, dust lingering ghostly in July air.

And across the river old men and women always
seemed to be sitting on their front stoops, watching.

And my brother once found a bat wedged beneath
the eaves of our house, hiding in full daylight.

Some nights the moon sank so low above the corn
it seemed to founder, gone to shoal, and once

I saw a red fox carrying in its mouth a dead field
mouse, the rodent twitching until the fox shook

it to remind it it had died. The smell of wet grass
prowled by the cistern where the exposed bone

of evening lined the ridge. And always the crows
had their secrets. Original crows, the darkness

of their wings lifting in air. Formed from rich,
black loam, calling methodically into the conspiracy

of wind, or appearing bitter above us, sharp wings
cutting sky. Sometimes the cries came closer, the feathers

darkly beautiful. And the nights were bruised flowers,
moonlight's estuary feeding its mouth into

the field: marrow-white, severed, falling bodily
to grass, the hours as permeable as clay.

ANCIENT WORLDS

My mother would tell of being
poor as mud as a child, of how

everyone, then, was fortunate even
to eat. But now, in better days,

she fed crows meat scraps from
our back porch, the dark bodies

flitting and moving through air,
rising from the field or rowing

out from the trees with dark
oars. The rocks were slippery

in the river behind our house,
and once I fell there and witnessed

the original blood of the world,
how it seeped into the moving

waters then disappeared. I heard
crows calling from their bodies,

heard my mother calling
for them to make an occultation

in the yard, and I returned
to the house to find them swirling

around her like a living veil.

GRAVITY

    As a child I wondered how prayers,
    lifting from a pew,

    made their way through stained glass.
    Was God perched

    in Heaven like a Great Blue Heron,
    thin-legged, patient?

    And nights I woke to Mother and Father
    arguing in the walls,

    voices sloshing like sudsy water.
    From my window I could watch

    the wind like a great broom
    sweeping through tall grass,

    disappearing into darkness
    like the blown pupil of an eye.

    And by day I watched the divinity
    of trees, and heard, on Sundays,

    church bells throbbing, making of the air
    a great reverberation,

    the way I imagined, at age ten or twelve,
    sex as something incorporeal, a moon

    outside a window or the small skull
    and scattering of bones I found

one December morning buried
in the hard mud beside the stream,

defleshed so otherworldly. And I closed
my hands around the hymnal

and envisioned prayers forming a certain
shape, or sleeping in

the hollow of a hickory. Perhaps they came
to love the earth so would not rise,

becoming like hornworms hiding the green
of their bodies amid

my mother's tomato plants.
And I imagined the moist silage

of breath inside my lungs, waiting there
to emerge, someday, in prayers.

DIASPORA

In Turner's *Sun Rising*
through Vapour:

Fishermen Cleaning
and Selling Fish,

the eye moves
without fail

from the clutter
of the human—

this compact labor—
to the sprawling

whorls and smudges
and smears

of old sky.
Once as a child

in Wisconsin, I handed
grape soda to a bear

on a chain, and the smell
of the animal body

was as familiar as the grass
I mowed each summer

up and down our yard's hill,
watching, as I did,

an older girl two houses over
who sunbathed daily

on a towel, and died—
I later learned—

when a train struck
a car at a railroad crossing

in distant Colorado.
And although

we'd never spoken,
I grieved for weeks,

believing I'd known
her once the way a bear

lifts a soda bottle
in its paws, and sunlight

can't quite tell itself
from morning clouds.

NOTES ON BEAUTY: *THE SKULL*

And in Turner's *Sun Setting
over a Lake,* the colors fuse

and bleed out
of the imagined

body of water and sky.
I believe this is

dumb substance,
evolving or devolving,

the way my father
used to love

the edge of woods
that looked out on the fence

and river. Here a day moon
lay broken above

a plumage of black-eyed
Susans. Or say

that moon was stone
and the grass was forever,

the way grackles
each morning

cry out their augury
from summer-thickened

leaves alive with
motion, and the mud

with its rank smells
has its divinations,

and at dusk
the bats row

out of the willows,
the old meditation

of moonlight scavenging
around us after dark,

sepulchral. Our father said
he went there to be alone,

to watch the hemoglobin
cars moving past

on the distant road,
to hear not his family

but primitive birds
singing from the old

church cemetery,
to watch, in winter,

a calligraphy
of snow chalking

the paper birches
like a faint solder

of moonlight.
And once he found

there a woodchuck's skull
half-buried

in the earth,
and he brought it

back to the house,
washed it with

a hose, wrapped it
in a box,

and presented it
to our mother

for their final
anniversary.

I was there
when she lifted it

into view—the most
strangely surprising

and beautiful gift
I'd ever seen.

ARS POETICA WITH HERON AND DANCE

In the years we lived overlooking the Monahegnee River,
there was a heron I spotted often in the shallows,
usually with only the stillness of its long legs
to keep it company. The creature gazed at the muddy waters
in the manner that snow studies the land toward which it falls,
mindless and singular in focus, without
the encumbrances of mercy. And if loneliness some summers
became the willows with their dreadlocks, I rose early
to sit at the kitchen table with my notebook,
words attempting sometimes to be sutures
and other times a scalpel. In those days solitude
seemed like the steep hill of grass I mowed across
the neighbor's lawn when I was twelve, mowed
because my parents commanded it as charity.
The elderly widow who lived in the stucco house
behind drawn curtains was dying, which gave
the wisps of her white hair—drifting sometimes like desultory
clouds beyond the windows—a mysterious dignity.
I was told it was breast cancer that was claiming her,
and so my legs strained into the incline of the hill,
my resentment at the chore tempered by my sense
of righteous purity, as though sweat staining a T-shirt
can become a form of holiness. There was something
in the exhaustion of calves and the steeped smells
of cut grass that seemed not an antidote to death
but its companion, as though all of life is the arduous digging
with our shovels into the earth we know will hold us.
Later that summer the dying woman's teenage granddaughter
came to visit, and she sunbathed sometimes on the patio,
the black of her bathing suit reminding me of the grackles
in the woods beyond the hill, birds always swooping
and sewing their feathers through the trees, birds
like the sounds of something rushing toward you

in a dream—so many flutterings of wings, such a commotion
of need. I remember watching her one day while she lay
on her stomach and read, her legs raised behind her
at the knees, entwined at the ankles and swaying,
as though this were the first human dance. Death seemed
to me, then, as far away as moonlight, which grazed
the earth in our backyard with its pale lips but still
belonged to another place and time, and was as ghostly
as the way, at dusk, the grackles in the trees gave way
to bats, as though everything transforms in darkness
to something ancient. I wanted the granddaughter to watch
my passage on the hill, wanted it in the manner that,
so many years later, I hoped the words I wrote above
the Monahegnee River would make of me a lonely spectacle,
would afford me even a portion of the dignity
of the heron existing as statuary in muddy waters.

FANFARE

When my father disappeared
finally with the crows,

I listened to a Norfolk Southern
emerging each night from

the darkness, like a mystical beast
or demigod, and grew as lonely

as the coyotes ghosting the field's
edge with their low-slung bodies.

And I wore the skin of dreaming,
the sounds of crickets intangible

in grass, the dusk sky slitting
the throats of the clouds.

And, come summer, water
flooded the river bank,

claiming possession of the field.
I tried to be the low-slung

clouds skimming the land
but never touching, and I listened

for the syntax of immensity,
summoned the geography

of raindrops offering
the smallness of their need

against the roof.
And still my thoughts

were wasps slipping in
and out of the paper hive.

My mother told me that certain
sounds were memories,

were sewn shut like a mouth
or maybe eyes. And I watched

the sky shirr the last faint stars
into pale gray, a bloom of ice

making stone come winter
of the river, the wind naming

the land the way the earth
dreams a coming fluency of snow.

FEAST AND FAMINE

Even after remarrying,
my father left in my mother's basement

a stuffed owl and his Civil War books.

The owl had glass eyes, and the dusty books
contained bloody illustrations of soldiers.

I was lonely that winter,
and I touched my fingers to the red smudges

on the page, watched out the upstairs windows
the white frock of snow covering everything,

watched the juncos and finches flutter
for position at my mother's feeder.

In the basement was my father's rolled-up print
of *The Old Guitarist,*

and once I saw my mother spread it out
on the concrete floor, study the long

fingers with their weary occultations,
the bent blue neck with its sorrowful beauty.

Then it was summer, and at night I spotted
teenage lovers carrying their blankets

through the backyard,
heading down to the river's edge.

The moon spoke to the grass in its salt voice.

And one night I dreamed
I heard the owl crying through the floorboards,

imagined it was a stone figure or obelisk.
Then, in the vision, the owl lifted itself

from the mud and desiccated grass,

became a dark stain moving
through the woods and toward the river,

brushing the naked branches going past.

SKINNY DIPPING

The water was black. We were sixteen.
We had our demarcations of river and sky,

the stars growing clumsy above us.
So we made a map of tongues, the fingerprints

of moonlight dusting grass where we spread
the blanket by the water's edge. It seemed

we were invisible inside our skin. And if love
was the praising of the small-scale hour,

here were our primitive breaths. And later—
carried by the current—we swam undressed,

our bodies no more anatomical than the stars.
And when it snowed come winter, the ground

became a kind of plumage, the great
white wing of a sleeping bird.

SONG OF PRAISE

Because I was seventeen
that summer

and dreamed my thoughts
came swarming

from the burning hive
of the night's sky,

that there was something
sharp and bitter

forever at the back
of my throat,

I ran before dawn
with my eyes closed,

the thin waves
of the reservoir praising

the moon with its
blessing of immense

mindlessness. The doctor
described for us

how a mind
slips loose

of its moorings,
how a day

becomes a dream
of pushing a wheelbarrow

into a river, watching
the water collecting

until the whole
contraption sinks.

I sat evenings with my
mother on the porch

and poured two
fingers of bourbon

in her glass. The yard's
grass swayed

to the rhythm
of forgetfulness.

A constellation
of starlings became

a neurological firestorm.
I ran that summer

until the need
for breath became

inconsolable
inside my lungs.

I imagined that
the lingering moon

was a jar of fireflies
the heavens carried

like a lantern, that soon
the bruise of dawn

would slip its necklace
of blood over

the horizon's neck.
I was a theorist, then,

of the lonely dark waters
I was circling. I thought,

Soon I will disappear.
I thought,

*Soon the world will split
open like a cracked egg.*

CROW ART

What begins? Forgets?
The weeds sway today

like scythes beside the river.
A lingering moon

presses one stirrup
into the hill's slope.

There is no oracle here,
just a few primordial clouds

drifting above the abandoned
kiln in the neighbor's yard,

slipping above the sprawl
of vases, plates, and porridge

bowls hardened by the fire.
At nineteen I moved across

the street from a funeral
home. Always there were

men and women in dark
clothes in the parking lot,

grief becoming half-veiled
moments witnessed out

a window, the attenuated
self. The sky was external

and isolated, the cars
in the lot with their mutable

shapes. But today, slowly,
the field's gray continent

is becoming, at its verge,
a faint flame, softening

into two smudges of crows
emerging from night's hall.

Here is the language of
relinquishment, my neighbor

firing up his kiln, smoke
corkscrewing into air to form

what appears, from a distance,
to be wisps of feathers, wings.

HOW HUMANS CAME TO LOVE

First rain overwhelmed
the creek, scratching earth.
You could sense the years
were eyelids opening
then closing. You could watch
in the primitive field—
beyond where the waters
slipped—a homily of stars
congealing after dark.
It was cold when the black
winds arranged themselves
across the plains. And there,
in a faint depression
of bare ground, two shadows
huddled close, the human
warmth conserved between
them soundless and discursive.
Soon the clouds dissolved
to expose the moon's
extracted tooth.
In the distant trees
a lost creature began
crying out its death agony.
The shadows stirred
faintly in their dreams,
slipping closer—the way
a rock dropped into
dark waters disappears.

BIRTHMARK

I come from
a beautiful country

with a bounty
of sutured fields

and a possum's
skull I unearthed

one summer
in the garden.

And each summer
my father used to cast

his fishing line
into the river,

and lovers, after dark,
carried blankets down

to the water's edge
beneath a clemency

of clouds. My father
spoke sometimes

of a German soldier
he shot in the neck

during WWII,
who fell into

a French river.
But now, at twenty,

I study a
woodpecker high

in the gray body
of a tree, the bird

tapping a secret
message into air.

And here on
my girlfriend's shoulder,

clinging like a root
or epidendrum,

is a birthmark—
dark-suited, beautiful—

a smudge like a bird
with its mysterious body.

WINTER SCHOOLS

And always we were reading,
books strewn like clouds
across the couch and coffee table.
Here was a blueprint for the body
in repose, our thoughts the tall grass
through which we waded,
this bundling come winter into
sweatpants and wool socks as we sat
before the fire, consuming words.
Sometimes we read on our bellies or on
the floor, or we lay in bed with the page's
syntax, and woke each morning to tangled
legs and books that had fallen to the floor
or were tucked beneath our pillows.
And we turned the pages in a slow pulse,
the words with their fallow ploughlands
waiting like the space between heartbeats
or breaths, a living abeyance while you stepped
from a shower and dried the cuneiform
tangles of your hair. The world outside
was slowing in the cold, congealing as still
and as hard as ice, the ground wanting
to find the permanence of stasis.
Then you draped your legs across my lap
and together—and separately—we read.

DUST DAY

Here is a bird's shape,
its geometries of movement

that seem no more significant
than a dust devil swirling past a willow.

There are always the questions
of equivalences: is the mud in the field

the same basic substance as the clouds,
the same as the air inside the lungs?

In my early twenties I was briefly
alone once more, the apartment's

back window looking out on an open field,
the front to dark cars and dark clothes

and a ceaseless gathering of mourners.
I sat evenings on the bed and wrote to you

about feeling like the discarded skin
of a snake left as an empty bracelet

on the grass. And each time I glanced out
one window there was gray smoke lifting from

the funeral home crematorium,
out the other a freight of gray clouds

drifting above the distant river.
Is the body's smoke the same

as the entrails of a catfish,
as the sound of a hearse lumbering

its complaint along a road?
Once I watched a hawk swoop low to the grass,

reach down the hook of its talons,
lift from the field a snake.

The writhing creature must have been amazed:
finally the world was giving way beneath it.

And before you had driven off,
you had left a pair of sandals

I perched as a reliquary
on the window sill.

I wrote from my bed
that we are complicit in dust, are the dark

wings of the distant birds, the drifting
outlines of a life.

And what if our hands
are the discarded skin of a snake?

To love like that, to wear the emptiness
of the bracelet all around us.

DIVINING MUD

Slowly the first dull grays of day
are making of the streambed

an augury of slop and matted grass.
It is here where I began, was conjured

from ghost mud and ghost weeds,
crawled out from the hollow end

of a decaying log. It is here where I lived
for many years, ranging past the fence where,

in winter, blood drops appeared across
the snow. Once I found the carcass

of a dead coyote, bloated at its belly,
the glass eyes opened into nothing.

But now, in a moment, I will make my way
back through dense woods and leave

my boots by our back door, caked heavy
with earth, will clean the dog's paws

with a green towel—then will find you still
in bed, your breaths lifting their revelations.

THE BODY'S MUD

My brother raised the question, at sixteen,
how anyone might make love to the same person

for a lifetime, suggesting, in his tone,
that years were a basin of water into which

the body cleansed itself for decades, the sloshing
liquid growing ever more muddy and fouled.

But today, at the base of the creek that stops
at the edge of the woods along our property,

my wife is lifting rich loam in shovelfuls
to carry in the wheelbarrow back to the garden,

where tomatoes will later grow
in such profusion we won't know how

we might ever consume them all.

PRAYER FOR STONES

The souls of migrating geese exist
for a moment in the air.
I would hold them there for longer
like a wisp of a cloud, if not for this rake
and the sounds it makes in the fallen
leaves, sounds like a conversation
that turns back forever on itself.
In our early years of marriage,
my wife returned again and again
to the topic of the miscarriage,
as though you might construct
a funeral pyre from so many repeated
consonants and vowels. Often I watched
the pattern of words against her lips,
shadows of stasis and movement,
as though they resembled the earliest
form of prayer, as ancient
as the first stone artifacts. You might say
the geese are praying, too, mostly
because they head out all in one
direction, the pelvis with its open V
giving birth to sky, the squawking
of the passage one more sorrowful
release. The first humans must have
imagined that birds ferried spirits
to their new home. At the hospital my wife
held my hand, the way the first
mother must have watched original grass
sway before her, must have felt
the lungs of a primal wind blowing out
across a landscape it had made.

BOTTOMLANDS DEPARTURE

This must be the place where sorrow goes,
here where mud clings and dusk pools

in the lowlands in September. A few weeks after
she lost the child—in the sixth month—

my wife and I lay one night on a hammock
in the backyard, and she told me how,

as a girl, she had wondered if prayers
ever grew trapped in their passage

in the hair of the clouds or the hook
of the moon. And soon the sepulchral

moon itself appeared amid the trees,
and I thought of the ghost milk

produced once by a childhood dog
after not one in her litter was born alive.

My wife leaned closer while the stars
grew slowly mired in their jar of formalin,

and alluvial darkness pressed down
close to the land. Our bodies, we know,

are obedient to time. And, as night steeped
around us with its murky tea, I closed my eyes

and thought of how soon it would be winter,
how snow would fall soundlessly in darkness,

would seem invisible, even while we heard
the lamentations of wind slipping

across the carapace of frozen land. And I felt
my breaths rising and falling in unison

with my wife's, and I thought of how it seems,
sometimes, that it snows inside the body.

DREAMING OF GOLDEN FLOWERS

This moon isn't dancing
in the courtyard

of the dead tonight, as Lorca
wrote, but dusting

the grass near the river
beyond our back fence

where young lovers
have spread their blanket

not far from where,
last summer,

our neighbor's horse
was shot in

the hindquarters
by passing teenagers

in a pickup.
Sometimes I stand

by the fence
and offer the horse

an apple cupped
in my palm,

and sometimes lovers
arrive after dark

to lie down by
the river amid

moonlight. We have
our animal bodies,

after all, like the children
who ran past

the doorway from which
Lorca was taken

by the Falangists.
I think we stutter

our way toward beauty,
which is why this field

tonight is blank
of everything except

the lovers, the horse,
and the loneliness

of moon and mud
and grass.

FERAL MOON

Once, as a child, my wife dreamed of obedient mud. How far away
the body was from grass, from the grievous claims

of the moon and stars. Now the earth divides itself into solitude
and years. Summer drags on. Some boys swerve on the highway

to murder an innocent turtle or raccoon. This is the sacrifice
we carry in the crucified hours. The dead

in some cultures are left out and exposed to the elements.
This is how we fade away to nothing. One moon

becomes another becomes a thousand. We are wild in our fear
of stories of unborn children who are lost.

Once humans made their existence from the mud. Once they gave
birth to the earthly movements of their tongues.

MOON LETTERS

When my wife sees our son throwing stones
into the river, she imagines the moon after dark

floating with a certain buoyancy above her,
the grass outside the windows covering the yard's

open mouth. Every field at first light becomes
an elegy: insects lifting from the swales,

clouds thin as starving horses, the river's mud
weaving through the milkweed and sumac.

And she carries the strata of the years like an ache
each time she thinks of our first boy we lost

in her sixth month, her belly for so long afterwards
a ghostly blossoming. And she watches after dark

how the moon whitewashes sorrow, lacquering
the shadows on the grass. We come to this out of our

bodies, she knows, a cloud's breath drifting
slowly overhead, ripe with rain that cannot bring

itself to fall, the hours sifting like embalming fluid
through our limbs, burrowing inside bones that are

hollowed out, tunneled with grief, black flowers
in night's garden. Then morning arrives once more,

annotated by birdcalls. There is a grackle with
dark eyes, a shapelessness of wind across

the field, each hour conjuring voices,
the sun performing its morning

ablutions. These are our bodies and our smoke,
our sprung notes becoming emptiness,

the years as lonely as a tuft of a weed.

BURYING

NOMADS

Every time I walk here
with this black ground
beneath me and the old hills
with their bald backs
and the skyways of dust
on the steep road up to the cemetery
with the moon at night that is a cracked
shell of sky, I think of doorways
opening into caverns and root cellars
and mouths in trees and doorways
inside of years where it seems
that a life is the paleness behind
the closed lid of any eye,
or the door where lovers shut
themselves away or one where
they cry out what might be prayers
or might be doves, and doors of history
and rivers, and the messengers
of *now* and *now* like the old men along
the river bank and the door where
their bobbers float, while some doors
are shadows or breaths or an oracle
of evening light or the kind of fire
that burns itself into such smoke
it billows up into a door,
and the river like a door where
the neighbor boy drowned,
and the door of weeks becoming
years then decades, and then there are bats
that make of a backyard
so many dark handkerchiefs
of doors, and soon there is a door
of plenty and a door of forgetfulness,

and only then do I realize it is possible
to fall into the pit of it,
and the door of ashes
you hold like something dissolving
in a palm, and the door
like a struck match
or a word that clings
to a tongue and will not fall,
or the door that is the grasslands
where the first nomadic humans
are walking and walking, and we
are waiting for it to open into us.

UNBLESSING

Mit allen Augen sieht die Kreatur
das Offene.
—RAINER MARIA RILKE

>   Here in the photograph are the remnants
>   of my father's Escanaba childhood
>   home, destroyed when an attic fan sparked
>   in the wiring and flamed up in laborious
>   August heat, leaving only a skeletal brick
>   fireplace to scale the sky's ladder.
>
>   And you can see—or almost see—summer
>   dusk waiting beyond the ruins, hidden in
>   the field, holding up the world.
>
>   And when I first lived with my wife in Ohio,
>   we could spy from our back windows, half-hidden
>   in the field where the land was receptive
>   to shadows, a road where, we later learned,
>   a boy had been struck and killed two years earlier.
>
>   It is the Huron who used to leave their dead
>   for many years above the ground, defleshed,
>   wrapped in animal skins; and poor Hermes,
>   born in a cave on Mount Cyllene, made music
>   with cow intestines and tortoise shells.
>
>   Some believe the heavens endure in silence,
>   while others imagine that what waits above us
>   is a great, protective room, a night vista
>   scabrous with stars.

Here is the hidden heart, I think,
prefigured, the sky at night unmoored,
the collusions of light and shadow
that make the world where we are living.

In my father's photograph there are stacked
fireplace bricks my great-grandmother said
were eventually carted away by men of no means—
hoboes, she said—men beyond hope in this
world except for what might be scavenged.

WINTERING

The secret of joy is the mastery of pain.
—ANAÏS NIN

    Here where the sun is cold,
    my father, wrapped in

    a wool blanket, is sitting
    on a back porch

    with its copse of plastic
    chairs around a glass table,

    near garden pots with
    shriveled flowers,

    his weathered hands splayed
    before him pale as grubs.

    He is telling stories
    of his memories from

    Escanaba, Michigan,
    where he was raised during

    the Great Depression
    by his grandmother, who ran

    a rooming house and despaired
    of being able to feed herself

    or her young charge. Later,
    in the War, my father was shot

by a sniper beneath his collarbone,
the bullet traversing through

his shoulder blade, and still
he carried himself with what

he imagined was an admirable
slump, as though you might wear

the precise scars of the world
against your body. As a boy

he broke into houses for food,
and he remembered standing

one evening at an upstairs window
with his grandmother, watching

a horse being butchered by
neighbors for their sustenance.

It seemed the memory
was formed from mud,

old as the first field,
as the blood he saw

on his neighbors' clothes
as they cut away

bright slabs of meat
in falling snow.

MOTHER

Here she is again, standing in
the winter yard, dark and frenzied

wings around her, the tin plates
of peanuts and meat scraps

set before her, the frozen creek
watching with its glass eye.

Come summer I will study
the muddy river's patience,

will make a prayer of earthly
bones, the congealing green skin

of the shallows in dead summer.
But for now there is only the banked

prayer of a snowdrift, the dusk
sun with its blood-red entrails.

The cold days are opening and closing
their insect eyes, and everywhere

wings flutter. And what of
the black obelisks as the crows arrive,

a sewn-shut sky that will give way
soon to an optic nerve of moon,

to the feathers catching and clinging
in dreams to my mother's hair?

LONG MARRIAGE

We see—from our bedroom window—the sky

undressing in morning light, the field's eyelid

slowly opening. And always we are older in our skin,

this life of rising in the gray then sipping coffee, the old snow

descending from the patient sky come winter, the ice softening,

each spring, at its center, turning darker, the weak sun

appearing as a canker amid the gray. And though the fields

when we were young had names, we address them now

like the palliative stars that emerge after dark, or like the shadows

of the clouds—by day—caressing the lawn outside this window,

speaking in the tender language of relinquishment.

NINE CROWS

There were nine crows in nine days
watching from the shadows amid the trees.

Black birds with black eyes, their folding
wings shrouded and thrashing blind

and corrosive—shadow stains—the creatures
cawing like breaking glass. Death was

the papery hive on the back porch, a maple
broken at its back, a rumor of stars and a catechism

of snake and sky. Later there was dust
on the window sill, a cellar lined with mason

jars—something listing milky and mysterious inside.
And always the crow woman of my memories

with her salves of celandine and musk flowers,
a thick green muck congealing atop the creek,

crabapples falling then decaying—dream fruit
blossoming into crows and foulmouthed

spells, the birds climbing into the amniotic light
toward a dilated moon roseate and clothed

in mist across the sky's open sore.

REVIVAL

I am listening this morning
to the bullfrogs and the sparrows,

while gazing out the upstairs window
at the prison a half mile down the road,

the hours inside those walls, my father
used to say, not sanded down along

the edges. I remember, when he was dying,
how he told me that the only music

he'd ever truly loved was the drumbeat
of the big guns of the destroyers

in the War. Last night I dreamed
of bullbats rising into a dark sky,

a bile of clouds above the hickories.
Here was the loneliness of grass

that would dull yellow come winter
in a cutting wind. And as for the prisoners,

I see them milling by the fence, imagine
that their voices are dust swirling

in a field. At night, I suspect,
they lie awake and listen to their breaths,

or dream of sunlight drifting fluted
into water, or imagine that they exist

inside a memory, in the nerve
endings of stars after dark.

PAPER SKIN

Today a cold wind is blowing through these open windows,
billowing the curtains, reminding me of how my father,

even in winter, disdained coats or hats or gloves
or even sweaters, believing in shirtsleeves, in the same way

he believed that a lighter for a cigarette was an affectation,
that wine was for the stuck-up rich and the weak-minded,

and indoor work wasn't actually any labor at all. He told me once
that the only true meats were beef or pork or venison, the last

preferably from a deer you shot yourself and dressed
with a knife slicing from crotch to sternum, the dark

blood welling. And he helped the ancient neighbor woman
carry groceries from her car, and he commanded me

to mow her grass in summer and shovel her driveway in winter.
She invited us more than once into her house for Coke

and doughnuts and once for a chocolate cake that had ants
she couldn't see swarming across the frosting. Another time

she fell on her front stoop and the paper skin along her elbow
and arm tore so badly that my father had to drive her

to the hospital. And when she died a year and a half later,
and before her relatives could make it down from Minnesota,

he had me use the spare keys to unlock her basement and shed doors, and to help him carry from her property to our own the tools

and electrical equipment that had once belonged to her dead husband, but now fit without complaint in our garage.

TOUCH

I grow old today like the unused garage door swollen stuck
in summer. This is our atonement for beauty. It is

proportional, sorrow, how the jays call to us with
the body's blue flash near where my wife used to garden.

We take our flesh and make of it one hundred drums,
erase the body's mud. And if I tell myself

I prepare for death in the soapy smell of my hands
as I dry them with a towel, I dream the rain dyes the grass

a darker green, staining it with a congress of touch, making of it art
that later, evaporating without fanfare, returns to air—

with the same ease that come January
this door will fall back open to my hand.

BLACK FLOWERS

These old men are dreaming of black flowers. They are springing from the earth, down in the oldest part of the woods, or growing from the skin of the trees. And then, by day, the men rise from bed and make their way onto the back porch. It is here where wind unfurls its cloak, undressing the earth, tousling the grass. The men have their memories as hymnals, but still the crows make blossoms of their wings, and oar out above the yard, speaking in tongues. Sometimes grandchildren come to visit, and the old men hold the young ones in their laps and speak of how, in August, dust can swirl up in a field until it almost seems to form a human shape. Occasionally the wives will sit for a few moments with their husbands, mostly in silence, the moon's straight-edged razor slicing into the empty body of the sky. But mostly the men have the smoke of the clouds to keep them company, clouds that turn white by day, to blood at dusk, to ash and then black flowers in the dark.

WINTER SNOW

The images are so faint now
I'm sure only of the far-off voice

of a classmate asking her—it must
have been fourth or fifth grade,

in homeroom—why she was sick all
the time, always blowing her nose,

always sniffling. And I know her face
was as pale as the snowstorms

that were forever arriving
the winter we rode the same bus.

She sat across from me or behind me
or in front of me, and my impression

was of the gray char of day, a purgatory
of frenetic white outside the window.

In high school she dated a brother
of my best friend, and I saw them

kissing once at the ice rink in Collier Park.
Her nose was pink with cold,

and she kept running a mitten beneath
it, and later I watched her skate

awkwardly below the sky's dark
mirror. I heard a rumor

that she had an abortion in her first
year of college, and I saw her one summer

in shorts, bare feet, and a T-shirt,
walking along the shoreline

of Lake Michigan. I know we spoke
briefly about our lives, but what

I remember are the sluggish waves
washing with determined adamancy

around us. I heard she married
after that, had two children, divorced,

moved to Arizona, moved back
to Illinois, then took her life in

her childhood bathroom. But none
of that is real, of course, none of that

stays. I hear her sniffling in the far-off
class, dabbing the Kleenex to her nose,

hear the voice rising up, accusatory,
and I see her shrugging in her seat, and later

see her kissing my friend's brother
beneath a black orchard of winter sky.

MUD EULOGIES

The old women of my dreams
stand at the windows in gray light,

gripping the sills and gazing
at the liver-spotted

backs of their hands.
And they study

the clouds' bandages
drifting past, study

the moon slipping loose
of its skin. Here is

a covenant of leaves
with dappled stains of light,

breaths like heat lightning
on a far-off horizon.

And if once children
sprang from the loam

of their bodies, now the stars
barely blink in the dark,

and the beggarly moon
hoards its myopia of longing.

And they rise each morning
in albino light, look out

to the manifold weeds
blooming at the yard's edge.

CONFESSION OF BATS

Because the hickory tree was close
to the house and hollowing,
my father brought it down,
releasing two bats to flee
into the air. Other bats flew
nightly above our fields at dusk,
praising the sky, and once,
in bright day, I saw one squeeze
behind a loose strip of bark
in another hickory by the barn.
My mother and brother impaled
half oranges on the chain-link fence
to entice orioles, which I dreamed
as a boy transformed to bats
after dark. And nights when
I was seventeen, I studied
the silage of stars decaying after
dark, the moon like a flowerpot left
and forgotten on a back
porch. Loneliness assembled
itself from the distant calls
of jays in the woods,
from the glass edges
of the sky, from the erratic
and drunken flight of the bats.
Years later, when I was married,
I had surgery for a detached retina,
and the gas bubble appeared to my sight
like a swimming pool's
receding surface. All of life
is taken from us, after all,
spooling out like rural Ohio
roads, as straight as railroad tracks.

And when my father was dying,
he dressed in a wool sweater
in summer's heat, and sat on
the back porch watching the cursive,
low-slung clouds and the dark
specks of bats as night approached.
Once he fell asleep beside me while
the baptismal fields beyond the fence
were burning at dusk. It was quiet as he slept,
and come morning, when I rose
from bed and walked out into
the backyard, day was a mouth pressing
down, a larynx of light slipping
out between the trees.

MAP OF THE WORLD

Last night you returned to me
in a dispatch of wind, a febrile rain.

And today a contusion of starlings
lifts from the field where two deer

bow their heads in supplication.
This must be the old heart of it,

the silentium where the dead go
when we are dreaming. I remember

a trip we took one August when newly
married, dust lifting across the road

as though to form a human shape.
We stayed in a cabin by a congealing

lake that seemed, each night,
like the dark pupil of an eye.

The lodge's owner, we were told,
had a son who was dying

at the hospital of leukemia.
By day we went swimming

in the brackish waters, and you told me
you were praying for the boy

we did not know, that the prayers
were like the leaves floating around

us in the shallows, or the four blind,
pink field mice we found one evening

nestled in the open grass,
or the miscarriage of moon

rising above the woods each night.
Now, today, the years seem sewn

shut and so forgotten. But tonight
I will leave on the light on the back porch,

leave the years to their own devices.
Come here, moonlight, I will think,

and sit with me. And we will dream
of a wind rising in the old fields,

the weight of it rustling through leaves
that are not ghosts but want to be.

NAMING THE FIELD

The boy who drowned in the river
is a locked door. You can see where

the deer lie down amid the grass,
see the constellations of the weeds.

And a fallen tree trunk by the fence
is hollowing at its center the way

the years move on without us. We name
each storm gathering above the woods,

name each raven swooping low, talons ready.
And the boy must have named the water

slipping into his lungs, named the current
carrying him off. The problem

with memory is that it can't tell itself
from snow coming down in winter,

from owl calls at night or a lone fox
at twilight trotting off into the trees.

The house where the boy lived
must lie just beyond the bridge and road,

and we name the smoke rising from
the chimney, name the field stretching

out in the direction of the water,
which excavates the earth beneath it.

The boy's name is the narrow verge
where the horizon is not quite sky

and not quite land, the snakeskin
I found one morning clinging to a wire

fence. Once, I imagine, I saw the boy skipping
stones across the muddy current

with his father, and the stones named
the loam when they sank to the bottom,

and the river named the stones, and the loam
named the river rushing over it.

www.ingramcontent.com/pod-product-compliance
Lightning Source LLC
Chambersburg PA
CBHW030123170426
43198CB00009B/717